Faye Dunaway's life and Career Story

The truth behind the Actress life and going through Bipolar health difficulties

Marty Woolery

Copyright © 2024 By Marty Woolery

All rights reserved. No part of this publication may be reproduced, distributed, or transmitted in any form or by any means, including photocopying, recording, or other electronic or mechanical methods, without the prior written permission of the publisher, except in the case of brief quotations embodied in critical reviews and certain other noncommercial uses permitted by copyright law.

Table of Contents

Introduction — 6
- Overview of Faye Dunaway's Career — 6
- The Stigma of Mental Health in Hollywood — 11

Chapter 1: The Iconic Rise — 20
- Early Life and Acting Beginnings — 20
- Breakthrough with Bonnie and Clyde — 24
- Success in Network and Other Films — 26

Chapter 2: The Dark Side of Stardom — 32
- Hollywood's Label: "Difficult" Star — 32
- Relationships and Public Perception — 38
- The Impact of Media and Public Scrutiny — 43

Chapter 3: Unraveling the Mystery — 49
- The Hidden Struggles: Alcoholism and Mental Health — 49
- The Misconceptions about Faye Dunaway — 53
- The Journey to Self-Awareness — 57

Chapter 4: The Bipolar Revelation — 62
- Faye Dunaway's Bipolar Diagnosis — 62
- The Decision to Go Public — 64
- The Role of Bipolar Disorder in Her Career — 67

Chapter 5: The Cathartic Documentary — 72
- Behind the Scenes of the Tell-All Documentary — 72
- Key Moments and Revelations — 75
- Public and Industry Reactions — 78

Chapter 6: The Role of Bipolar Disorder in Art — 82
- Understanding the Mania and Sadness — 82
- How Mental Health Influenced Dunaway's

Performances	85
The Intersection of Creativity and Mental Health	88
Chapter 7: Overcoming the Stigma	**93**
Faye Dunaway's New Understanding of Herself	93
The Importance of Mental Health Awareness in Hollywood	95
Lessons Learned and Shared	99
Conclusion	**103**
Reflecting on Faye Dunaway's Legacy	103
The Ongoing Dialogue About Mental Health in the Entertainment Industry	106
Looking Ahead	110
Appendices	**113**
Timeline of Faye Dunaway's Career	113
Key Interviews and Sources	114

Introduction

Overview of Faye Dunaway's Career

Faye Dunaway is an iconic figure in Hollywood, whose career spans several decades and includes some of the most memorable performances in film history. Born Dorothy Faye Dunaway on January 14, 1941, in Bascom, Florida, she grew up in a strict, military family. This upbringing, marked by discipline and constant movement, instilled in her a resilience and determination that would later fuel her rise to stardom. Dunaway's early interest in acting led her to study at the University of Florida and later Boston University, where she honed her craft and prepared herself for the competitive world of theater. Her Broadway debut came in 1962 with *A Man for All Seasons,* which set the stage for her transition to film. Her beauty, combined with a fierce intensity, made her a standout performer, and it wasn't long before Hollywood took notice. Her breakthrough role came in 1967 when she starred as Bonnie Parker in *Bonnie and Clyde,* opposite Warren Beatty. The film, directed by Arthur Penn, was a groundbreaking piece of cinema that not only redefined the crime genre but also cemented Dunaway's status as a major star. Her portrayal of the infamous outlaw was both charismatic and chilling, earning her an Academy Award nomination for Best Actress. The film's success marked the beginning of a stellar career that would see Dunaway take on a variety of challenging roles.

Throughout the 1970s, Dunaway continued to build on her early success with performances that showcased her range and depth as an actress. In *The Thomas Crown Affair* (1968), she played a sophisticated, chess-playing insurance investigator opposite Steve McQueen. Her performance in *Chinatown* (1974), directed by Roman Polanski, remains one of her most celebrated. As Evelyn Mulwray, she embodied the classic femme fatale, a woman of mystery and tragedy, navigating a web of corruption and deceit in 1930s Los Angeles. This role further solidified her reputation as one of the most talented actresses of her generation. Dunaway's career reached new heights with *Network* (1976), a satirical drama that critiqued the television industry. Her portrayal of Diana Christensen, a ruthless TV executive who would stop at nothing to achieve ratings success, earned her the Academy Award for Best Actress. The role was a perfect fit for Dunaway's commanding presence, allowing her to explore themes of power, ambition, and the moral cost of success. *Network* was both a critical and commercial success, and Dunaway's performance remains a high point in her career. Despite these triumphs, the 1980s brought significant challenges. Dunaway starred in *Mommie Dearest* (1981), a biographical film about the life of Joan Crawford, based on the memoir by Crawford's adopted daughter, Christina. Dunaway's portrayal of Crawford was intense and unflinching, depicting the actress as a domineering and abusive mother. While the performance was lauded by some, the film itself was panned by critics and has since become infamous for its camp value. The role had a lasting impact on Dunaway's career, as she struggled to escape the shadow of the character and the negative press that followed. The 1990s and 2000s saw Dunaway take on fewer roles, but she continued to work in both film and television, often choosing projects that allowed her to explore new facets of her talent. She also made her directorial debut with the short film *The Yellow Bird* (2001), showcasing her desire to expand her artistic horizons. Dunaway's later career, while not as prominent as her earlier years, demonstrated her enduring passion for acting and her commitment to her craft.

Throughout her career, Faye Dunaway has been known for her intense, emotionally charged performances. She has portrayed a wide range of characters, from the glamorous to the deeply troubled, often bringing a complexity to her roles that resonated with audiences. Her work has been recognized with numerous awards, including an Academy Award, three Golden Globe Awards, and a BAFTA. Despite the ups and downs, Dunaway's place in Hollywood history is secure, and her influence on the art of acting remains profound.

The Stigma of Mental Health in Hollywood

While Faye Dunaway's career is marked by incredible highs, it has also been accompanied by personal and professional challenges, many of which are linked to the stigma surrounding mental health in Hollywood. This stigma, prevalent not only in the film industry but across society, has historically made it difficult for actors and other creative professionals to speak openly about their mental health struggles. In Hollywood, where the pressures of fame, public scrutiny, and the demands of the industry can be overwhelming, mental health issues are not uncommon. However, the fear of being labeled "difficult" or "unstable" has often led actors to hide their struggles, leading to a culture of silence and denial. This has been particularly true for women in the industry, who face additional pressures related to ageism, sexism, and unrealistic beauty standards. For many years, mental health was a topic shrouded in secrecy, with few willing to discuss it openly. The stigma of mental health in Hollywood has deep roots, dating back to the early days of the film industry. The myth of the "tortured artist," whose genius is inextricably linked to their suffering, has long been romanticized. This narrative suggests that mental illness is a necessary component of creativity, rather than a serious health issue that requires attention and care. As a result, many actors and creatives have felt compelled to endure their struggles in silence, fearing that revealing their condition could jeopardize their careers. Faye Dunaway's experiences are a reflection of this broader issue. Throughout much of her career, she was labeled as "difficult," with stories of on-set conflicts and temperamental behavior frequently making headlines. These accounts contributed to a perception of Dunaway as a challenging figure to work with, overshadowing her talent and achievements. In reality, much of this behavior was likely connected to her struggles with bipolar disorder, a condition that was not publicly acknowledged until much later in her life.

Bipolar disorder is characterized by extreme mood swings, including periods of mania and depression. For those in the public eye, the effects of this disorder can be exacerbated by the relentless demands of their profession and the constant scrutiny of the media. In Dunaway's case, her manic episodes may have fueled the intensity of her performances, while the depressive phases likely contributed to the difficulties she faced in her personal and professional life. However, without a clear understanding of her condition, these behaviors were often misinterpreted as signs of a difficult personality. The stigma surrounding mental health has also been perpetuated by the media, which has historically sensationalized the struggles of celebrities. Stories of breakdowns, addictions, and erratic behavior have been used to sell tabloids, often without regard for the well-being of the individuals involved. This type of coverage not only reinforces negative stereotypes but also discourages others from seeking help for fear of being similarly judged. In recent years, there has been a gradual shift in how mental health is perceived in Hollywood and society at large. Increased awareness and advocacy have led to more open discussions about mental health, and many celebrities have come forward to share their experiences. This shift has been partly driven by a broader cultural movement toward destigmatizing mental illness and recognizing it as a legitimate health issue that deserves attention and care. Faye Dunaway's decision to speak publicly about her bipolar disorder is part of this larger trend. By revealing her diagnosis, she has helped to shed light on the challenges faced by those living with mental illness and has contributed to the ongoing conversation about mental health in the entertainment industry. Her openness has allowed for a re-examination of her career, providing context for behaviors that were previously misunderstood or misrepresented.

The importance of addressing mental health in Hollywood cannot be overstated. The pressures faced by actors and other creatives are unique, and the impact of these pressures on mental well-being can be profound. In an industry where image is everything, the fear of being perceived as weak or unstable has often prevented individuals from seeking the help they need. However, as more people speak out and share their experiences, the stigma surrounding mental health is gradually being eroded. The shift in perception is also reflected in the types of stories being told in Hollywood. Films and television shows are increasingly exploring themes related to mental health, offering more nuanced and empathetic portrayals of characters dealing with mental illness. This change not only reflects a growing awareness of the issue but also contributes to a broader cultural understanding of mental health.

Faye Dunaway's career is a testament to her incredible talent and resilience. However, it also highlights the challenges faced by those living with mental illness in an industry that has historically stigmatized mental health. By speaking openly about her bipolar disorder, Dunaway has helped to challenge these stigmas and has played a role in the ongoing effort to create a more supportive and understanding environment for mental health in Hollywood. As the conversation continues to evolve, it is essential that the industry and society at large continue to move toward a more compassionate and informed approach to mental health, one that recognizes the humanity of those who struggle and provides the support they need to thrive.

Chapter 1: The Iconic Rise

Early Life and Acting Beginnings

Faye Dunaway was born Dorothy Faye Dunaway on January 14, 1941, in Bascom, Florida, a small rural town near the Georgia border. Her father, John MacDowell Dunaway Jr., was a career non-commissioned officer in the United States Army, and her mother, Grace April, was a homemaker. As a military family, the Dunaways moved frequently, which meant Faye grew up in various parts of the country, including Texas, Utah, and Germany. This transient lifestyle imbued Dunaway with a sense of discipline and resilience, qualities that would later become crucial in her demanding career in Hollywood.

Despite the constant moves, Dunaway was a diligent student and developed an early interest in the arts. Her passion for acting was sparked during her high school years, where she participated in drama productions. She was drawn to the idea of embodying different characters and exploring the human condition through performance. After graduating from high school, she attended Florida State University, where she initially studied education. However, her love for acting led her to transfer to Boston University, where she pursued a degree in theater. At Boston University, Dunaway immersed herself in the study of drama, training under esteemed teachers who recognized her potential. She was particularly influenced by Professor Edwin Grover, who encouraged her to pursue a career in acting. Dunaway's time at Boston University provided her with a solid foundation in the craft of acting, and she soon began to audition for professional roles. Her first break came in 1962 when she was cast in the Broadway production of *A Man for All Seasons*, directed by Robert Bolt. Although her role was small, it was an important stepping stone that introduced her to the world of professional theater. Dunaway's performance caught the attention of critics, and she began to build a reputation as a talented young actress. She followed this with appearances in other stage productions, including *After the Fall*, written by Arthur Miller, in which she played the lead role of Maggie. This role, which was loosely based on Marilyn Monroe, allowed Dunaway to explore complex emotional territory and demonstrated her ability to convey vulnerability and strength in equal measure. By the mid-1960s, Dunaway had established herself as a promising actress on the New York stage, but she was eager to transition to film. Her striking looks and intense performances made her a natural fit for the screen, and it wasn't long before Hollywood took notice. Dunaway made her film debut in 1967 with *The Happening*, a comedy that, while not a major hit, marked her entry into the film industry. However, it was her next role that would catapult her to stardom.

Breakthrough with Bonnie and Clyde

Faye Dunaway's breakthrough came with her role as Bonnie Parker in the 1967 film *Bonnie and Clyde*. Directed by Arthur Penn and produced by Warren Beatty, who also starred as Clyde Barrow, the film was a game-changer for Hollywood. It was a bold and innovative film that redefined the gangster genre, blending elements of comedy, drama, and violence in a way that had never been seen before. Dunaway was cast as Bonnie Parker after an extensive search for the right actress to play the role. The character of Bonnie required a unique combination of charm, toughness, and vulnerability, and Dunaway embodied all these qualities. Her portrayal of Bonnie was both seductive and menacing, capturing the complexity of a woman who was both a lover and a criminal. Dunaway's performance was magnetic; she brought a sense of danger and excitement to the role that captivated audiences. Bonnie and Clyde was a commercial and critical success, and it became one of the most influential films of the 1960s. The film was nominated for ten Academy Awards, including Best Picture, and Dunaway received her first Oscar nomination for Best Actress. Her performance as Bonnie Parker made her a star overnight, and she quickly became one of the most sought-after actresses in Hollywood.

The success of *Bonnie and Clyde also marked a turning point in American cinema. The film's depiction of violence, its anti-establishment themes, and its unconventional narrative structure influenced a new generation of filmmakers and paved the way for the New Hollywood movement of the 1970s. Dunaway's role in the film not only defined her career but also left an indelible mark on the history of cinema.

Success in Network and Other Films

Following the success of Bonnie and Clyde, Faye Dunaway's career continued to ascend. She took on a variety of challenging roles that allowed her to showcase her range as an actress. In 1968, she starred opposite Steve McQueen in *The Thomas Crown Affair*, playing a sophisticated insurance investigator. The film was a stylish heist thriller that featured one of the most iconic chess scenes in cinema history. Dunaway's performance was lauded for its elegance and wit, further establishing her as a leading lady in Hollywood. Dunaway continued to work with some of the most respected directors of the time. In 1974, she starred in Roman Polanski's *Chinatown*, a neo-noir masterpiece that is widely regarded as one of the greatest films ever made. Dunaway played Evelyn Mulwray, a mysterious and tragic figure entangled in a web of corruption and deceit. Her performance was both haunting and poignant, and she received widespread acclaim for her portrayal of a woman caught between loyalty and survival. The film was a critical and commercial success, earning eleven Academy Award nominations, including one for Dunaway as Best Actress.

However, it was her role in the 1976 film *Network* that would become one of the defining performances of her career. Directed by Sidney Lumet, *Network* was a satirical drama that explored the dark side of the television industry. Dunaway played Diana Christensen, a ruthless and ambitious television executive who will stop at nothing to achieve high ratings. Her portrayal of Diana was both chilling and compelling, as she embodied the cutthroat nature of the media industry.

Network was a critical and commercial triumph, and it won four Academy Awards, including Best Actress for Dunaway. Her performance as Diana Christensen remains one of the most memorable in film history, and it solidified her status as one of the greatest actresses of her generation. The film's exploration of media manipulation and the pursuit of power resonated with audiences and critics alike, and it remains relevant to this day.

Network, Dunaway continued to deliver powerful performances in films throughout the 1970s and 1980s. She starred in *Three Days of the Condor* (1975), a political thriller directed by Sydney Pollack, and *Eyes of Laura Mars* (1978), a psychological thriller in which she played a fashion photographer with a psychic connection to a series of murders. These roles allowed Dunaway to explore different genres and characters, showcasing her versatility as an actress.

However, her career took a controversial turn in 1981 when she starred in *Mommie Dearest*, a biographical film about the life of actress Joan Crawford, based on the memoir by Crawford's adopted daughter, Christina. Dunaway's portrayal of Crawford was intense and unflinching, depicting the actress as a domineering and abusive mother. While the performance was praised by some, the film was widely criticized and became infamous for its camp value. The role had a lasting impact on Dunaway's career, as she struggled to escape the shadow of the character and the negative press that followed. Despite the challenges, Faye Dunaway's contributions to cinema are undeniable. Her performances in Bonnie and Clyde, Chinatown, and Network are among the most iconic in film history, and they have left a lasting legacy. Dunaway's ability to bring depth and complexity to her characters has earned her a place among the greatest actresses of all time. Her journey from a small town in Florida to the heights of Hollywood stardom is a testament to her talent, determination, and resilience.

Chapter 2: The Dark Side of Stardom

Hollywood's Label: "Difficult" Star

Faye Dunaway's ascent to Hollywood stardom was meteoric, but with fame came the burdens of public scrutiny and industry pressures that would ultimately contribute to her being labeled a "difficult" star. This label, often applied to female actresses, particularly those who assert themselves in a male-dominated industry, has historically been used to marginalize and control women in Hollywood. For Dunaway, this label became an albatross that overshadowed her talent and contributions to the film industry.

The origins of Dunaway's reputation as difficult can be traced back to her early successes in the late 1960s and 1970s. As an actress who took her craft seriously, Dunaway was known for her intense dedication to her roles. She approached her work with a level of commitment that demanded high standards not only from herself but also from those around her. This perfectionism, while contributing to her brilliant performances, often led to clashes with directors, co-stars, and crew members.

One of the most notable instances that contributed to this reputation occurred during the filming of *Chinatown* in 1974. Directed by Roman Polanski, the film is now considered a classic, but its production was fraught with tension. Polanski, known for his meticulous and often abrasive directing style, frequently clashed with Dunaway. Reports from the set describe how the two would argue over everything from line readings to camera angles. Dunaway, who was deeply invested in her character, Evelyn Mulwray, wanted to ensure that every aspect of her performance was perfect. This dedication, however, was often interpreted as stubbornness or unwillingness to collaborate. The tension reached a peak during the filming of a pivotal scene where Dunaway's character is slapped by Jack Nicholson's character, Jake Gittes. According to various accounts, Polanski insisted on multiple takes to capture the perfect shot, leading to Dunaway becoming increasingly frustrated. The situation escalated to the point where Dunaway allegedly threw a cup of urine at Polanski after he refused to allow her a bathroom break. While this incident has become the stuff of Hollywood legend, it also reinforced the narrative of Dunaway as a difficult actress, a label that would follow her throughout her career. This reputation was further solidified during the production of *Mommie Dearest* in 1981. The film, a biographical account of actress Joan Crawford based on the memoir by her adopted daughter, Christina Crawford, was an emotionally and physically demanding project for Dunaway. Her portrayal of Crawford was intense, requiring her to tap into deep reservoirs of emotion to depict the abusive and controlling nature of the character. Dunaway later admitted that playing Crawford had taken a significant toll on her, both mentally and emotionally.

However, the grueling nature of the role, combined with the already high expectations placed on Dunaway as an actress, led to reports of difficult behavior on set. Crew members and co-stars described her as demanding and high-strung, and these accounts were eagerly picked up by the media. The negative press surrounding *Mommie Dearest* only served to reinforce the public perception of Dunaway as difficult, with the film's eventual cult status doing little to rehabilitate her image. In reality, Dunaway's so-called difficult behavior was likely a result of her intense passion for her craft and the immense pressure she felt to deliver exceptional performances. The label of "difficult" is often applied to women in the entertainment industry who refuse to conform to traditional expectations of femininity and subservience. For Dunaway, her assertiveness and desire for control over her work were misconstrued as problematic, whereas similar behavior in male actors might have been celebrated as dedication or artistic temperament. The impact of this label on Dunaway's career was significant. While she continued to work in Hollywood, the reputation of being difficult made it harder for her to secure roles, especially as she aged. The industry's inherent ageism, coupled with her existing reputation, meant that opportunities became scarcer, and she was often typecast in roles that did not fully utilize her talents. Despite her accomplishments, the "difficult" label became a shadow that loomed over her career, affecting not only her professional life but also her personal relationships and public perception.

Relationships and Public Perception

Faye Dunaway's personal life, like her professional life, was marked by intense scrutiny from the media and the public. Her relationships, in particular, were often the subject of tabloid headlines, further contributing to her complex public image. Dunaway's romantic life was tumultuous, with several high-profile relationships and marriages that played out under the watchful eye of the press. One of her most notable relationships was with actor Marcello Mastroianni, whom she met while filming *A Place for Lovers* in 1968. Mastroianni, an Italian cinema icon, was married at the time, but he and Dunaway began a passionate affair. Their relationship was marked by deep emotion and mutual admiration, but it was also fraught with challenges. Mastroianni, unable to leave his wife, offered Dunaway a life as his mistress, which she ultimately rejected. The end of their relationship left Dunaway heartbroken, and it would take years for her to fully recover. Dunaway's first marriage was to singer Peter Wolf, the lead vocalist of the rock band The J. Geils Band. They married in 1974, but their relationship was strained by their demanding careers, which often kept them apart. Dunaway's intense focus on her work, combined with the pressures of fame, created distance between the couple, and they divorced in 1979. Despite the separation, Dunaway and Wolf remained on amicable terms, with Dunaway later reflecting that their relationship had been a victim of their conflicting schedules rather than a lack of love. In 1983, Dunaway married British photographer Terry O'Neill, with whom she had a son, Liam. The marriage seemed to provide a period of stability in Dunaway's life, but it too was plagued by difficulties. The pressures of balancing her career and motherhood, along with O'Neill's work commitments, eventually led to the breakdown of the marriage. They divorced in 1987, and Dunaway would later describe this period as one of profound sadness and loss. The media's focus on Dunaway's relationships often overshadowed her professional achievements, reducing her to a figure defined by her romantic entanglements rather than her work. This focus was not unique to Dunaway; many actresses of her generation faced similar treatment, where their personal lives were scrutinized to a degree that their male counterparts rarely experienced. The constant attention to her relationships added to the perception of Dunaway as a troubled and difficult figure, further complicating her public image. Public perception of Dunaway was also shaped by her roles in film, particularly her portrayal of Joan Crawford in Mommie Dearest. The intensity and ferocity with which she played the character led many to conflate Dunaway with Crawford, believing that the actress shared the same temperament as the woman she portrayed. This confusion between character and actor was exacerbated by the media, which often blurred the lines between Dunaway's on-screen personas and her real-life behavior. Dunaway herself was acutely aware of the impact that public perception had on her life and career. In interviews, she spoke of the challenges of living under constant scrutiny and the difficulty of maintaining a private life in an industry that thrived on exposure. Despite these challenges, Dunaway remained fiercely protective of her privacy, choosing to keep much of her personal life out of the public eye. This decision, while allowing her some control over her image, also contributed to the perception of her as aloof or distant. The impact of media and public scrutiny on Dunaway's life cannot be understated. The relentless focus on her personal relationships, combined with the industry's labeling of her as difficult, created a narrative that often overshadowed her accomplishments as an actress. This narrative, however, was not entirely reflective of the real Faye Dunaway—a woman of immense talent, depth, and complexity who navigated the challenges of fame with resilience and grace.

The Impact of Media and Public Scrutiny

The media's portrayal of Faye Dunaway played a significant role in shaping her public image, often to her detriment. Throughout her career, Dunaway was subjected to intense media scrutiny, which frequently focused on her personal life and on-set behavior rather than her professional achievements. This scrutiny was not only invasive but also often sensationalized, contributing to a distorted perception of the actress. In the 1970s and 1980s, the tabloid press was at its peak, with publications like *The National Enquirer* and *The Star* dominating newsstands. These outlets thrived on scandal and controversy, often fabricating or exaggerating stories to sell copies. Dunaway, as a high-profile actress, became a prime target for these publications. Stories about her alleged on-set outbursts, romantic entanglements, and personal struggles were regularly featured, often with little regard for accuracy or fairness. The impact of this negative press on Dunaway's career was profound. The constant barrage of stories depicting her as difficult and troubled made it harder for her to secure roles, especially as she aged. The industry's already pervasive ageism was compounded by the media's portrayal of her as a problematic figure, leading to fewer opportunities and a decline in her career. For an actress of Dunaway's caliber, this was a bitter pill to swallow, as she saw her career opportunities diminish not because of a lack of talent but because of a narrative constructed by the media. Moreover, the media's portrayal of Dunaway had a lasting impact on her mental and emotional well-being. The constant scrutiny and negative press took a toll on her self-esteem and contributed to a sense of isolation. Dunaway, who had always been intensely private, found herself increasingly withdrawn from the public eye

, reluctant to engage with the media or discuss her personal life. This withdrawal, in turn, only fueled further speculation and gossip, creating a vicious cycle that was difficult to break. The media's treatment of Dunaway is reflective of a broader pattern in Hollywood, where female stars are often subjected to harsher scrutiny and more invasive coverage than their male counterparts. Actresses who assert themselves or refuse to conform to traditional expectations are frequently labeled as difficult or problematic, while their male peers are celebrated for similar behavior. This double standard has long been a part of the entertainment industry, and Dunaway's experience is a stark example of its consequences.

Despite these challenges, Dunaway's legacy as an actress remains intact. Her performances in films like Bonnie and Clyde, Chinatown, and Network are considered among the finest in cinema history, and her impact on the industry is undeniable. However, the media's role in shaping her public image serves as a cautionary tale about the power of the press and the ways in which it can influence not only an individual's career but also their personal life. In recent years, there has been a growing awareness of the need for a more balanced and respectful portrayal of women in the media, particularly in the entertainment industry. The rise of social media and the #MeToo movement have empowered women to speak out against the injustices they face and demand fairer treatment. For Dunaway, this shift represents a long-overdue recognition of the challenges she faced throughout her career, and a vindication of sorts for the struggles she endured. As society continues to grapple with issues of gender equality and media representation, Faye Dunaway's story serves as a powerful reminder of the need for change. Her journey, marked by incredible highs and devastating lows, is a testament to her resilience and strength. Despite the dark side of stardom, Dunaway's talent and legacy as an actress remain indomitable, and her contributions to film continue to inspire new generations of performers.

Chapter 3: Unraveling the Mystery

The Hidden Struggles: Alcoholism and Mental Health

Faye Dunaway, one of Hollywood's most celebrated actresses, faced a series of personal battles that remained hidden from the public for much of her career. While her talent was undeniable, Dunaway's life behind the scenes was marked by struggles with alcoholism and mental health issues that she kept private for many years. These struggles not only affected her personal life but also influenced her public persona and the way she was perceived by others in the industry.

Dunaway's issues with alcoholism began to surface during the height of her career. As the pressures of fame mounted, she found herself turning to alcohol as a coping mechanism. The constant demands of the industry, combined with the intense scrutiny from the media, created a perfect storm of stress and anxiety. Alcohol provided a temporary escape, allowing her to numb the emotional pain and maintain the image of the glamorous star the public expected her to be. However, as with many who struggle with addiction, the relief provided by alcohol was short-lived, and the consequences were devastating. Dunaway's drinking began to interfere with her work, leading to erratic behavior on set and strained relationships with colleagues. The same dedication and intensity that made her a brilliant actress became sources of internal conflict as she tried to balance her professional responsibilities with her growing dependency on alcohol. Adding to the complexity of Dunaway's struggles was her battle with mental health issues, which she later revealed included bipolar disorder. For much of her life, these challenges remained undiagnosed and untreated, leading to periods of extreme highs and lows. During her manic phases, Dunaway could be incredibly productive and energetic, channeling her emotions into her performances with astonishing results. However, the depressive episodes that followed were debilitating, leaving her feeling isolated, hopeless, and overwhelmed.

The intersection of alcoholism and bipolar disorder created a cycle that was difficult for Dunaway to break. The manic episodes fueled her drinking, while the depressive periods intensified her reliance on alcohol as a form of self-medication. This cycle took a significant toll on her personal and professional life, contributing to the negative perceptions of her as a difficult and unpredictable figure in Hollywood. Dunaway's struggles with alcoholism and mental health were further compounded by the stigma surrounding these issues, particularly in the entertainment industry. At the time, there was little understanding or acceptance of mental health disorders, and admitting to such challenges could easily derail a career. As a result, Dunaway kept her struggles hidden, maintaining a facade of control even as her life spiraled out of balance. This secrecy only served to deepen her isolation, as she was unable to seek the help and support she desperately needed.

The Misconceptions about Faye Dunaway

Throughout her career, Faye Dunaway was often misunderstood and mischaracterized by the media and the public. The label of being a "difficult" star, which was applied to her early on, overshadowed many of the underlying issues that contributed to her behavior. This narrative was not only unfair but also failed to acknowledge the complexities of Dunaway's life and the challenges she faced behind the scenes.

One of the most persistent misconceptions about Dunaway was that her on-set behavior was the result of a demanding and controlling personality. In reality, much of her so-called difficult behavior was rooted in her struggles with mental health and the pressures of maintaining her status as a leading actress in Hollywood. Her perfectionism and intense commitment to her roles were often misinterpreted as diva-like behavior, when in fact they were a reflection of her desire to excel and her fear of failure. The media's portrayal of Dunaway also contributed to the public's misconceptions about her. Sensationalized stories about her alleged outbursts and difficult behavior were often taken at face value, with little consideration given to the context or the personal challenges she was facing at the time. This one-dimensional portrayal ignored the complexities of her character and the fact that, like many people, she was struggling with issues that were not immediately visible to the outside world. Another misconception about Dunaway was that she was aloof and unapproachable. This perception was partly due to her reserved nature and the protective barriers she erected around herself to shield her from the constant scrutiny of the public and the press. However, those who knew her well often spoke of her warmth, intelligence, and generosity. Dunaway was deeply passionate about her craft and cared deeply about the people she worked with, but the pressures of fame and the need to protect herself from the harsh realities of the industry often made it difficult for her to express these qualities openly. These misconceptions were further exacerbated by the lack of understanding of mental health issues at the time. The symptoms of bipolar disorder, such as mood swings, irritability, and periods of intense energy, were often misinterpreted as personality flaws rather than manifestations of a mental health condition. This lack of awareness contributed to the negative perceptions of Dunaway and prevented her from receiving the empathy and support she needed. It is important to recognize that the narrative of Faye Dunaway as a difficult and troubled star is a product of its time, shaped by societal attitudes towards mental health, addiction, and the roles of women in the entertainment industry. While Dunaway's struggles were real and had a significant impact on her life and career, they were often misunderstood and misrepresented by those who did not have the full picture.

The Journey to Self-Awareness

Despite the challenges she faced, Faye Dunaway's journey towards self-awareness and acceptance is a testament to her resilience and strength. Over the years, she gradually came to terms with her struggles with alcoholism and mental health, and took steps to address these issues and reclaim her life. One of the key turning points in Dunaway's journey was her decision to seek help for her alcoholism. Recognizing that her drinking was having a detrimental effect on her life, she made the difficult decision to enter rehabilitation. This decision marked the beginning of a new chapter for Dunaway, as she committed herself to sobriety and the process of healing. Through therapy and support from those around her, she began to gain a deeper understanding of the factors that had contributed to her addiction and learned healthier ways to cope with the pressures of her career and personal life. In addition to addressing her alcoholism, Dunaway also sought treatment for her bipolar disorder. This diagnosis provided her with a framework for understanding the emotional highs and lows she had experienced throughout her life. With the help of mental health professionals, Dunaway was able to develop strategies for managing her symptoms and maintaining stability. This journey towards self-awareness allowed her to recognize the importance of self-care and the need to prioritize her mental health, even in the face of the demands of her career. Dunaway's journey was not an easy one, and it required her to confront painful truths about herself and her life. However, it also allowed her to gain a deeper sense of self-acceptance and to let go of the shame and guilt that had haunted her for so many years. Through this process, she was able to reclaim her identity and redefine her relationship with her work and the industry that had both celebrated and vilified her. In recent years, Dunaway has been more open about her struggles, sharing her experiences in interviews and documentaries. This openness has not only helped to destigmatize issues of mental health and addiction but has also allowed Dunaway to take control of her narrative. By speaking out about her journey, she has been able to challenge the misconceptions that have surrounded her for so long and to offer hope to others who may be facing similar challenges. Dunaway's journey to self-awareness is a powerful reminder of the importance of resilience and the capacity for growth and change. Despite the many obstacles she faced, she was able to confront her demons and emerge stronger on the other side. Her story is one of courage and perseverance, and it serves as an inspiration to others who may be struggling with their own challenges. In the end, Faye Dunaway's legacy is not defined by the struggles she faced, but by her ability to overcome them. She remains one of Hollywood's most iconic actresses, and her journey towards self-awareness is a testament to the power of determination and the human spirit.

Chapter 4: The Bipolar Revelation

Faye Dunaway's Bipolar Diagnosis

Faye Dunaway's revelation of her bipolar disorder was a defining moment in her life, both personally and professionally. For decades, the actress had struggled with intense emotional highs and lows, often manifesting in ways that were misinterpreted by those around her. It wasn't until later in life that Dunaway was diagnosed with bipolar disorder, providing a crucial explanation for much of her behavior and experiences over the years. The diagnosis was both a relief and a challenge for Dunaway. On one hand, it offered a framework to understand the mood swings and erratic behavior that had characterized much of her life. On the other hand, it forced her to confront the reality of living with a mental health condition that, at the time, was heavily stigmatized and often misunderstood. This diagnosis was not just about putting a name to her experiences; it was about coming to terms with a condition that had profoundly shaped her life and career. Bipolar disorder, characterized by periods of mania and depression, can be particularly challenging for those in high-pressure environments like Hollywood. The manic phases can lead to heightened creativity and energy, while the depressive phases can result in deep despair and withdrawal. For Dunaway, this meant that her career was a rollercoaster of brilliant performances and moments of intense personal struggle.

The diagnosis allowed Dunaway to look back on her life and see how bipolar disorder had influenced her actions and decisions. It also gave her the tools to manage her condition better and seek the help she needed. However, the journey to this point was not easy, and it required immense courage to face the truth about her mental health.

The Decision to Go Public

The decision to go public with her bipolar diagnosis was not one Dunaway took lightly. For years, she had been labeled difficult, temperamental, and unpredictable—a reputation that had followed her throughout her career. Revealing her diagnosis was a way to set the record straight, but it also meant exposing a deeply personal aspect of her life to the world. Dunaway's choice to share her diagnosis was driven by a desire to reclaim her narrative and provide context for the public's perception of her. She understood that by revealing her struggles with bipolar disorder, she could help others understand the complexities of mental health and reduce the stigma associated with it. In doing so, she hoped to inspire others facing similar challenges to seek help and not feel ashamed of their condition. The decision was cathartic for Dunaway, allowing her to lift the burden of secrecy that had weighed on her for so long. In interviews, she spoke candidly about the relief she felt in finally being able to share her truth and how it helped her make sense of her past. By going public, Dunaway was not only advocating for herself but also for a broader understanding of mental health issues in the entertainment industry and society at large. This revelation also marked a turning point in how Dunaway was perceived. While some continued to view her through the lens of her past, many began to see her in a new light—as a person who had faced significant challenges and had the strength to confront them openly. Her courage in sharing her diagnosis helped to humanize her and shifted the narrative from one of a "difficult" star to that of a resilient individual who had faced her struggles head-on.

The Role of Bipolar Disorder in Her Career

Bipolar disorder played a significant role in shaping Faye Dunaway's career, both in terms of the performances she delivered and the challenges she faced along the way. The condition's characteristic mood swings—ranging from manic highs to depressive lows—had a profound impact on her work, influencing everything from her choice of roles to her on-set behavior. During her manic phases, Dunaway experienced bursts of energy and creativity that allowed her to deliver some of the most intense and memorable performances of her career. These periods of heightened emotion and focus were critical to her ability to inhabit complex, often emotionally charged characters. Films like Bonnie and Clyde and Network showcased her ability to channel her inner turmoil into powerful, nuanced portrayals that captivated audiences and critics alike. However, the flip side of these manic episodes was the depressive phases that often followed. During these times, Dunaway struggled with feelings of hopelessness and exhaustion, which made it difficult to maintain the same level of performance and professionalism. These lows were often misunderstood by those around her, leading to the perception that she was unreliable or difficult to work with. In reality, Dunaway was grappling with the effects of a mental health condition that she did not fully understand at the time.

The pressure to maintain a public image of perfection in Hollywood only exacerbated the challenges posed by her bipolar disorder. Dunaway felt the need to hide her struggles, fearing that any sign of weakness could jeopardize her career. This constant pressure to appear strong and composed added another layer of stress, making it even harder for her to manage her condition effectively. Despite these challenges, Dunaway's bipolar disorder also gave her a unique edge in her performances. The intensity of her emotions, driven by the condition, allowed her to tap into deep reservoirs of empathy and understanding, bringing a raw authenticity to her roles. This emotional depth became a hallmark of her acting style, setting her apart from her peers and earning her a place among the greatest actresses of her generation. In the later years of her career, with her diagnosis in hand, Dunaway began to approach her work with a new sense of self-awareness. Understanding her condition allowed her to manage her symptoms more effectively and make choices that prioritized her mental health. This newfound balance enabled her to continue working in the industry she loved, while also advocating for greater awareness and understanding of mental health issues. Ultimately, Faye Dunaway's revelation of her bipolar disorder was not just a personal milestone; it was a moment of public significance. By sharing her story, she helped to break down the stigma surrounding mental health in Hollywood and beyond. Her willingness to confront her challenges publicly demonstrated the importance of self-awareness and resilience in the face of adversity. Dunaway's legacy, therefore, is not only one of remarkable talent but also of courage and strength in the face of life's most difficult challenges.

Chapter 5: The Cathartic Documentary

Behind the Scenes of the Tell-All Documentary

The creation of Faye Dunaway's tell-all documentary was a deeply personal and transformative experience for the iconic actress. After decades of being branded as one of Hollywood's most difficult stars, Dunaway saw the documentary as an opportunity to reclaim her narrative and offer a more nuanced portrayal of her life and career. The project was not just another biographical account; it was a cathartic journey that allowed Dunaway to confront her past and share her truth with the world.

Behind the scenes, the documentary was a collaborative effort between Dunaway and a select team of filmmakers who were committed to telling her story with honesty and sensitivity. Dunaway was involved in every aspect of the production, from selecting archival footage to shaping the narrative arc. This level of involvement ensured that the final product was not only accurate but also deeply reflective of her personal experiences. The documentary's production was marked by several emotional moments as Dunaway revisited her past. The process of going through old footage, interviews, and personal mementos was both painful and liberating. It required Dunaway to confront the most challenging periods of her life, including her struggles with mental health, her tumultuous relationships, and the public's perception of her as a difficult and temperamental star. Despite the emotional toll, Dunaway was determined to present an unflinching portrayal of her life, believing that transparency was essential to achieving the documentary's goals. The filmmakers faced the challenge of balancing the darker aspects of Dunaway's life with her professional achievements. While the documentary did not shy away from exploring her struggles, it also celebrated her contributions to cinema and her enduring legacy as one of Hollywood's greatest actresses. This balance was crucial in ensuring that the documentary was not just a recounting of past scandals but a comprehensive exploration of Dunaway's life, career, and the complexities that defined both.

Key Moments and Revelations

The documentary featured several key moments and revelations that offered new insights into Faye Dunaway's life and career. One of the most significant revelations was her admission of having bipolar disorder, which she had kept private for many years. This revelation provided a critical context for understanding much of her behavior throughout her career, including the emotional highs and lows that had often been misunderstood by the public and the media. Another poignant moment in the documentary was Dunaway's candid discussion of her struggles with alcoholism. She spoke openly about how alcohol had served as a coping mechanism during the most challenging periods of her life, particularly when dealing with the pressures of fame and the intense scrutiny of the public eye. Her honesty in discussing these issues highlighted the toll that addiction and mental health struggles can take on even the most successful and seemingly untouchable individuals. The documentary also delved into Dunaway's relationships, both personal and professional, offering a more nuanced perspective on her interactions with others in the industry. While Dunaway acknowledged that she had been difficult to work with at times, she also provided context for her behavior, explaining how her mental health struggles and the demands of her career had contributed to her actions. This nuanced portrayal helped to humanize

Dunaway, showing her not just as a star but as a person who had faced significant challenges and had done her best to navigate them. One of the most powerful aspects of the documentary was Dunaway's reflection on her legacy. She spoke about the importance of her work and the pride she took in her performances, even as she acknowledged the personal costs of her career. This reflection offered a sense of closure, as Dunaway came to terms with her past and the impact it had on her life. It also underscored the importance of resilience and self-acceptance, themes that resonated throughout the documentary.

Public and Industry Reactions

The release of Faye Dunaway's tell-all documentary generated significant attention and sparked widespread discussion in both the public and the entertainment industry. For many, the documentary was a revelation, offering a side of Dunaway that had long been hidden from view. Her candidness about her struggles with mental health and addiction was particularly impactful, as it challenged the longstanding stigma surrounding these issues and highlighted the importance of compassion and understanding. Public reactions to the documentary were largely positive, with many viewers expressing admiration for Dunaway's courage in sharing her story. The documentary resonated with audiences on a personal level, as it addressed universal themes of struggle, resilience, and the pursuit of self-acceptance. Dunaway's willingness to be vulnerable and honest endeared her to many who had previously only known her through the lens of her public persona. Within the industry, the documentary prompted a reevaluation of Dunaway's career and legacy. While her reputation as a difficult star had long overshadowed her achievements, the documentary provided a more balanced perspective that allowed her contributions to cinema to be appreciated in a new light. Industry professionals, including directors, actors, and critics, praised the documentary for its depth and honesty, and many acknowledged that it had changed their perception of Dunaway.

The documentary also had a broader impact on the entertainment industry's approach to mental health. Dunaway's openness about her bipolar disorder and alcoholism helped to break down some of the barriers that had previously prevented discussions about mental health in Hollywood. Her story served as a reminder that even the most successful individuals are not immune to the challenges of mental illness and addiction and that these issues should be addressed with empathy and support rather than judgment. In the end, the documentary was not just a retrospective of Faye Dunaway's life and career; it was a powerful statement about the importance of owning one's narrative and confronting the past with honesty and courage. For Dunaway, it was a cathartic experience that allowed her to reclaim her story and redefine her legacy. For audiences and industry professionals alike, it was a poignant reminder of the complexities of fame and the resilience required to overcome life's challenges.

Chapter 6: The Role of Bipolar Disorder in Art

Understanding the Mania and Sadness

Bipolar disorder is characterized by extreme mood swings, ranging from manic highs to depressive lows. For those living with the condition, these swings can profoundly impact every aspect of life, including professional endeavors. In Faye Dunaway's case, understanding the role that these extremes played in her life provides a critical lens through which to view her work and her legacy as an actress. The manic phases of bipolar disorder are marked by heightened encrgy, creativity, and confidence. Individuals may feel invincible, driven by a sense of urgency to create or achieve. In contrast, the depressive phases bring profound sadness, fatigue, and a sense of hopelessness, often leading to withdrawal from activities and relationships. For Dunaway, these emotional extremes were not just personal struggles—they were integral to her artistic process. In her manic states, Dunaway likely found herself infused with the energy and intensity that allowed her to deliver some of the most powerful performances of her career. The emotional depth and complexity required to portray certain characters could be fueled by the heightened emotions associated with mania. However, the same manic energy that propelled her on set could also make her interactions with colleagues challenging, as her intensity might have been overwhelming to those around her.

The depressive phases, on the other hand, may have offered Dunaway a different kind of insight into the human experience—one rooted in pain, introspection, and vulnerability. These periods of deep sadness could have allowed her to connect with characters who were struggling with their own inner demons, bringing a raw authenticity to her performances that resonated with audiences. Yet, these depressive episodes also meant that maintaining the same level of performance and professionalism was an ongoing challenge, particularly in an industry that demands consistency.

How Mental Health Influenced Dunaway's Performances

Faye Dunaway's bipolar disorder undeniably shaped her approach to acting. The condition's mood swings provided her with a broad emotional palette from which to draw, allowing her to infuse her roles with a depth and complexity that set her apart from her peers. Whether consciously or unconsciously, Dunaway's performances were often reflective of her own internal struggles, with her characters embodying the extremes of emotion that she experienced in her personal life. In films like Network and Bonnie and Clyde, Dunaway's characters are marked by a fierce intensity that mirrors the highs of her manic episodes. Her portrayal of Diana Christensen in Network is a prime example of this, where she channels an almost manic energy into the character's relentless drive and ambition. The result is a performance that crackles with electricity, making Diana a compelling and unforgettable figure on screen. This same intensity can be seen in her portrayal of Bonnie Parker in *Bonnie and Clyde*, where Dunaway's raw energy brings a sense of danger and excitement to the character. Conversely, Dunaway's depressive states may have allowed her to tap into the more melancholic and tragic aspects of her characters. In roles where her characters are confronted with loss, despair, or existential crises, Dunaway's own experiences with depression may have provided a well of emotion from which to draw. This is evident in her portrayal of Joan Crawford in *Mommie Dearest*, where the character's inner turmoil and eventual unraveling are brought to life with a haunting authenticity. Dunaway's ability to convey the fragility and vulnerability of her characters likely stems from her own battles with these emotions, making her performances deeply relatable to audiences.

The interplay between Dunaway's mental health and her art is a testament to the complex relationship between creativity and mental illness. While her bipolar disorder undoubtedly posed challenges, it also contributed to the intensity and emotional depth that became hallmarks of her acting style. This duality—where her greatest struggles also became her greatest strengths—is a common theme in the lives of many artists who have grappled with mental health issues.

The Intersection of Creativity and Mental Health

The intersection of creativity and mental health is a subject that has long fascinated psychologists, artists, and scholars. The idea that mental illness, particularly conditions like bipolar disorder, can fuel creativity is a concept that has been explored in various studies and cultural narratives. Faye Dunaway's career offers a compelling case study in this intersection, where her experiences with bipolar disorder both hindered and enhanced her creative output. Mania, with its surge of energy and racing thoughts, can lead to bursts of creativity that are often unmatched by those without the condition. For Dunaway, these manic episodes may have provided her with the drive to take on challenging roles and the confidence to push boundaries in her performances. The rapid flow of ideas and heightened emotions associated with mania could have fueled her ability to connect with her characters on a profound level, resulting in performances that were both powerful and innovative. However, the link between creativity and mental illness is not without its complications. While mania can lead to great creative output, it is often followed by depressive episodes that can be debilitating. For Dunaway, the aftermath of a manic phase could bring about periods of deep sadness and withdrawal, making it difficult to sustain the creative momentum she had built. This cyclical pattern of highs and lows is common in artists with bipolar disorder, where periods of intense productivity are followed by times of inactivity or even despair. The broader implications of this intersection between creativity and mental health are significant. It challenges the romanticized notion of the "tortured artist" by highlighting the very real struggles that accompany mental illness. For every burst of creativity, there is often an equal or greater period of suffering, making the creative process both a gift and a burden for those with bipolar disorder. Dunaway's career exemplifies this duality, where her greatest artistic achievements are inextricably linked to her personal struggles with mental health. In the context of Hollywood, where the pressure to perform and maintain a public image is immense, the challenges posed by bipolar disorder are magnified. Dunaway's ability to navigate these challenges while still delivering some of the most iconic performances in film history is a testament to her resilience and talent. Her story underscores the importance of understanding and supporting mental health in the creative industries, where the demands of the profession can often exacerbate underlying conditions. Faye Dunaway's bipolar disorder played a pivotal role in shaping her career and her legacy as an actress. The mania and sadness that defined her condition also fueled her creativity, allowing her to bring a unique intensity and emotional depth to her performances. However, this intersection of mental health and creativity came with its own set of challenges, highlighting the complexities of living and working with bipolar disorder in the public eye. Dunaway's story serves as a powerful reminder of the intricate relationship between art and mental health, and the need for greater awareness and compassion in understanding this connection.

Chapter 7: Overcoming the Stigma

Faye Dunaway's New Understanding of Herself

In the latter stages of her career, Faye Dunaway's journey of self-discovery led to a profound new understanding of herself, particularly in light of her diagnosis with bipolar disorder. This revelation was not just a medical diagnosis but a key that unlocked many of the mysteries and challenges that had defined her life. For decades, Dunaway had been labeled as a "difficult" star, with her intense behavior and emotional volatility often misunderstood by those around her. However, with the clarity provided by her diagnosis, Dunaway was able to reframe these aspects of her personality, understanding them not as flaws, but as manifestations of her mental health condition. This new understanding brought with it a sense of relief and empowerment. No longer burdened by the labels that had been unfairly placed upon her, Dunaway began to see her life and career through a different lens. She recognized that many of the struggles she faced—both personal and professional—were influenced by her bipolar disorder. This realization allowed her to approach her past with greater compassion for herself, acknowledging the challenges she had faced and the resilience she had shown in overcoming them. Dunaway's new understanding also extended to her work as an actress. She came to appreciate how her bipolar disorder had influenced her performances, contributing to the emotional depth and intensity that characterized her most iconic roles. Rather than seeing her condition as a hindrance, Dunaway began to view it as a unique aspect of her artistic identity—something that had shaped her career in profound ways. This shift in perspective was crucial in helping her to reconcile her past and embrace her future with renewed confidence.

The Importance of Mental Health Awareness in Hollywood

Faye Dunaway's journey underscores the critical importance of mental health awareness in Hollywood, an industry notorious for its high-pressure environment and relentless demands. For too long, the entertainment industry has been a place where mental health issues are stigmatized, with actors and other professionals often reluctant to seek help for fear of damaging their careers. Dunaway's experience sheds light on the need for greater understanding and support for mental health within the industry. The entertainment world is one where appearances are paramount, and any sign of vulnerability can be perceived as a weakness. This culture of perfectionism often forces individuals to suppress their struggles, leading to a dangerous cycle of untreated mental health issues. Dunaway's story illustrates the toll that such an environment can take on individuals, particularly those with conditions like bipolar disorder, which are characterized by emotional extremes. Her struggles were exacerbated by the lack of understanding and support within the industry, leading to a cycle of misinterpretation and mismanagement of her behavior. In recent years, there has been a growing awareness of the importance of mental health in Hollywood, with more actors and filmmakers speaking out about their own experiences. Dunaway's decision to publicly share her diagnosis of bipolar disorder is a significant contribution to this movement. By revealing her struggles, she has helped to destigmatize mental health issues in the industry, encouraging others to seek help and be open about their own experiences. Her story serves as a reminder that mental health is not something to be ashamed of, but rather an essential aspect of overall well-being that should be treated with the same importance as physical health. This shift towards greater mental health awareness in Hollywood is not just about individual well-being; it's also about fostering a healthier and more supportive work environment. When mental health is prioritized, actors and other industry professionals are better equipped to manage the demands of their work, leading to more sustainable careers and, ultimately, better performances. Dunaway's journey highlights the need for ongoing education and support for mental health in Hollywood, so that future generations of actors do not have to face the same challenges she did.

Lessons Learned and Shared

Faye Dunaway's experiences offer valuable lessons for both the entertainment industry and the broader public. One of the key takeaways from her story is the importance of self-awareness and self-compassion. Dunaway's journey towards understanding her bipolar disorder was not an easy one, but it was a necessary step in her healing process. Her experience shows that coming to terms with one's mental health is a critical aspect of personal growth and well-being. Another important lesson from Dunaway's story is the need for greater empathy and understanding when it comes to mental health. For too long, mental health issues have been stigmatized and misunderstood, leading to isolation and suffering for those affected. Dunaway's openness about her condition has helped to challenge these stigmas, showing that mental illness is not a personal failing, but a health condition that requires care and understanding. Her story encourages others to approach mental health with compassion, both for themselves and for those around them. Dunaway's experience also highlights the role of resilience in overcoming life's challenges. Despite the many obstacles she faced—both related to her mental health and the pressures of her career—Dunaway remained committed to her craft and her personal growth. Her ability to continue working and to ultimately share her story is a testament to her strength and determination. This resilience is a powerful example for others facing similar struggles, showing that it is possible to overcome adversity and find meaning in one's experiences. In sharing her story, Dunaway has also contributed to a broader cultural conversation about mental health. Her decision to speak out about her bipolar disorder has helped to raise awareness and reduce stigma, making it easier for others to seek help and support. This is perhaps one of the most significant lessons from her journey: that by sharing our stories, we can help to create a more understanding and supportive world for everyone. Finally, Dunaway's experience serves as a reminder of the importance of seeking help. For many years, she struggled in silence, not fully understanding the nature of her condition. It was only when she sought professional help that she was able to gain the insights and tools needed to manage her bipolar disorder. Her story underscores the importance of early intervention and the benefits of therapy, medication, and other forms of treatment in managing mental health conditions. Faye Dunaway's journey of overcoming the stigma of mental health is a powerful story of self-discovery, resilience, and advocacy. Her new understanding of herself, coupled with her commitment to raising awareness, has not only transformed her own life but has also contributed to a larger cultural shift towards greater acceptance and support for mental health in Hollywood and beyond. Through her experiences, Dunaway has shared valuable lessons that continue to resonate with those facing similar struggles, offering hope and inspiration for a more compassionate and understanding world.

Conclusion

Reflecting on Faye Dunaway's Legacy

Faye Dunaway's legacy in Hollywood is undeniably complex, shaped by her towering achievements and the personal struggles that both fueled and sometimes overshadowed her career. From her breakout role in *Bonnie and Clyde* to her unforgettable performance in *Network*, Dunaway carved out a place in cinematic history as one of the most talented and intense actresses of her generation. Her ability to convey deep emotion and bring complex characters to life made her a force to be reckoned with on screen. However, Dunaway's legacy is not solely defined by her filmography. The revelations about her struggles with bipolar disorder add a new dimension to her story, casting light on the personal battles that accompanied her professional triumphs. Understanding her mental health challenges provides a fuller picture of the woman behind the roles, offering a glimpse into the vulnerabilities that drove her to greatness but also led to periods of turmoil. Dunaway's journey is a testament to the duality that often exists in the lives of creative individuals, where the very traits that contribute to their brilliance can also be sources of great pain. Her legacy, therefore, is one of both immense talent and immense struggle, and it invites a more compassionate understanding of the complexities of mental health in the context of a high-pressure industry like Hollywood.

As we reflect on Dunaway's career, it becomes clear that her impact extends beyond her performances. By sharing her story, she has opened up a crucial conversation about mental health, particularly in an industry that has long stigmatized and misunderstood these issues. Dunaway's decision to go public with her bipolar diagnosis is a courageous act that not only humanizes her but also contributes to a broader cultural shift towards greater empathy and awareness.Her legacy is now intertwined with this advocacy, marking her not just as an icon of cinema but also as a figure who helped to challenge the stigma around mental illness. In this way, Dunaway's life and career offer valuable lessons about resilience, vulnerability, and the importance of mental health awareness in all walks of life.

The Ongoing Dialogue About Mental Health in the Entertainment Industry

Faye Dunaway's public revelation about her bipolar disorder is part of a growing movement within the entertainment industry to address mental health more openly and honestly. For too long, Hollywood has been a place where mental health struggles were hidden behind the glamorous facade, often with devastating consequences. The pressures of fame, the demands of the industry, and the relentless scrutiny of the media create an environment where mental health issues can easily be exacerbated, yet seeking help has historically been seen as a sign of weakness.

However, in recent years, there has been a significant shift in how mental health is discussed and treated in Hollywood. More actors, directors, and other industry professionals are coming forward with their own stories of mental health challenges, helping to break down the stigma and encourage others to seek the help they need. This shift is crucial in creating a more supportive and understanding environment where mental health is treated with the same seriousness as physical health. Dunaway's story is an important contribution to this ongoing dialogue. By sharing her experiences, she has helped to normalize conversations about mental health, particularly bipolar disorder, which is often misunderstood and stigmatized. Her willingness to be vulnerable in the public eye serves as a powerful example for others in the industry, showing that it is possible to maintain a successful career while also managing a mental health condition. The entertainment industry, with its influence and reach, plays a crucial role in shaping public perceptions of mental health. As more industry figures speak out about their experiences, it helps to reduce the stigma and encourages a broader societal acceptance of mental health issues. This, in turn, can lead to better support systems, both within the industry and in society at large, for those struggling with their mental health. Moreover, the representation of mental health in films and television is also evolving. There is a growing recognition of the importance of portraying mental health issues accurately and sensitively, rather than perpetuating harmful stereotypes. This shift in representation can have a profound impact on audiences, helping to foster greater understanding and empathy for those dealing with mental health conditions. Dunaway's story is also a reminder of the importance of providing mental health support for those working in the entertainment industry. The pressures of the industry can take a toll on even the most resilient individuals, and it is essential that there are resources and support systems in place to help them navigate these challenges. This includes access to therapy, support groups, and other mental health services, as well as creating a culture where seeking help is encouraged and supported.

The ongoing dialogue about mental health in Hollywood is a positive step towards creating a more compassionate and understanding industry. However, there is still much work to be done. Stigma still exists, and many individuals continue to suffer in silence. It is essential that the industry continues to prioritize mental health and to advocate for greater awareness and support.

Looking Ahead

As we look ahead, it is clear that the conversation about mental health in the entertainment industry will continue to evolve. Faye Dunaway's story is just one of many that highlight the importance of this issue, and her courage in speaking out will undoubtedly inspire others to do the same.

By continuing to raise awareness and challenge the stigma around mental health, the industry can create a more supportive environment for all its members. Dunaway's legacy, therefore, is not just about her remarkable career as an actress, but also about her contribution to this critical conversation. Her story serves as a powerful reminder of the importance of understanding and addressing mental health, not just in Hollywood, but in all areas of life. It is a legacy that will resonate for years to come, helping to pave the way for a more compassionate and empathetic world. Faye Dunaway's journey from one of Hollywood's most iconic stars to an advocate for mental health awareness is a testament to her strength, resilience, and willingness to embrace her vulnerabilities.

Her legacy is a multifaceted one, encompassing her incredible contributions to film, her struggles with bipolar disorder, and her role in challenging the stigma around mental health. As the conversation about mental health in Hollywood continues to grow, Dunaway's story will remain a touchstone, reminding us of the importance of empathy, understanding, and support in all our lives.

Appendices

Timeline of Faye Dunaway's Career

- 1941: Born in Bascom, Florida.

- 1967 : Breakthrough role in Bonnie and Clyde, earning her first Academy Award nomination.

- 1976 : Wins an Academy Award for Network.

- 1981 : *Mommie Dearest* becomes a cultural touchstone, though critically mixed.

- 1990s : Faces fewer leading roles due to her "difficult" reputation.

- 2024 : Reveals her bipolar disorder in a tell-all documentary.

Key Interviews and Sources

- Larry King (1995): Dunaway reflects on her career and personal challenges.
- The New York Times (2008) : Discusses her reputation and industry challenges.
- RadarOnline (2024) : Dunaway reveals her bipolar diagnosis.
- Vanity Fair (2010) : Explores her legacy and personal life.
- *mDocumentary: The Real Faye Dunaway(2024): A deep look into her life and career.

Made in the USA
Coppell, TX
12 December 2024